Protect Your Family

Life Insurance Basics For Special Needs Planning

ROB WRUBEL, CFP®

ISBN 978-0996659208,

DEDICATION

My family is amazing and supports me every day. My three children, Benjie, Sarah and Annie, keep asking about the books I am writing and by doing so keep me motivated and inspired. I appreciate each day with them and delight in their energy, smiles and good cheer.

Kelly is a constant fan and her love and belief in me keeps me writing and inspired. Thank you for taking the time to make this book better.

My parents deserve a huge thank you and show of gratitude. They have been supportive of my ambitions and education all along the way.

Thank you to the team at Cascade Investment Group for their support and generosity. We have an amazing group of people that I get to work with each day. Theresa makes everything happen for me with grace and humor. We have a special work environment due to the efforts of everyone on our team - Ken, Dana, Felicia, Jan and Craig.

CONTENTS

BLUEPRINTS

I am the father of three children. My middle child is a beautiful girl with Down syndrome. Since her birth, I have worked to enjoy the wonderful new directions of life she brings to my family.

Financial planning looks different with her in my life than it did when I did not have a family member with special needs. Now, my family looks to access and protect government benefits along with our other plans for the future – retirement, education, travel and other life goals.

After her birth, I took time to understand the legal, social and financial aspects of our plan and how they work together. It is a complex area of planning. I created the Blueprints financial planning process to help families become motivated about making the best life possible. Blueprints is a comprehensive process to help families set goals for the future, protect available government benefits, get out of debt and invest for the future. It is designed to help each of your family members live the most fulfilling life possible.

Families with special needs members have unique planning considerations. We have family members who will need our support while we live and will still need support after we pass away. We need to build the best financial lives for ourselves. We have to get the right legal plans in place. We need to understand the government benefits we can access and the organizations that can support our family members in the future.

Our plans must incorporate the potential for government benefits like Supplemental Security Income and Medicaid-funded services.

Blueprints has nine Building Blocks to follow. The process uses the metaphor of building a house. Houses do not get built overnight.

i

The plan requires moments to dream, then specific actions to get the best foundation in place.

The Building Blocks:
1. Dreaming About Your Future
2. Starting To Design
3. Taking Stock
4. Building A Foundation – The Special Needs Trust
5. Eliminating Debt Forever
6. Financial Stability
7. Protect Your Family
8. Investing For Your Future
9. Funding The Trust

Life insurance is part of Building Block 7 – Protect Your Family. It is the most important insurance for families to have as they save and invest for the future.

Unfortunately, too many people buy the wrong type of life insurance to help them protect their families. They buy policies they cannot afford that do not create enough value in the case of an unexpected death.

This Building Block is the one people least like to discuss. But it is one of the easiest to get in place – all it takes is a few meetings and the process gets started.

This book hopes to show you why you should start with term life insurance – the simplest and easiest type to understand. If all you do is review your coverage and put term life insurance in place then this book has done its job. There are other types of life insurance that might be useful down the road and these are reviewed. Some families buy other types of insurance if they are out of debt, have saved for retirement and created financial stability. They are not recommended for families who have not taken care of the first eight Building Blocks.

INTRODUCTION

This book seeks to answer the question I get from families with a special needs member, "Did I buy the right type of life insurance?" It seems like a simple question that deserves a simple answer: yes or no. Next question? But why do so many people buy life insurance they cannot afford, does not meet their protection needs and does not create enough wealth for their families?

Life insurance comes in different types of wrappers and there is an emotion to buying insurance that complicates how people buy it.

The basic concept of life insurance starts with the desire to take risk out of a family's life. We use small dollar premium payments to create a pool of money in the event of an untimely death. This is the purpose of insurance at its core. Health insurance. Disability insurance. Car and home insurance. In all cases, we pay monthly premiums to protect ourselves in the event of a catastrophe. Car insurance replaces the car or pays to get it fixed. We cannot afford to rebuild a home lost to fire – the homeowner's insurance is in place to do that.

Life insurance should be the same. We should use it to cover potential losses at those times where the losses are otherwise unaffordable. That's it.

For some reason, life insurance has a set of options that do not exist in health, car and home insurance. Life insurance policies can have account values and investments. They can be used as investment accounts similar in some ways to 401(k) accounts, Roth IRAs and taxable investment accounts. Some types of life insurance are sold to fund specific future goals and not just to protect against the loss of a family member. They are sold with an emotional pitch and a tax pitch that obscures the basic protection role.

This book seeks to help you sort out fact from fantasy and to give you the tools to determine the best type of life insurance for your family. It takes the main types of policies on the market and gives you side-by-side comparisons on how the policies work and the values you might expect to have using a real example.

Families working through the Building Blocks must focus on protection while building a strong financial life. Families like ours must think about caring for our family member with special needs even after we are gone. This involves putting the right building blocks in place – a strong estate plan, assets to support quality of life in the future and a care plan for daily living.

The dollars we use to fund those future plans come from savings today. They can be invested or spent in many ways. Those savings can be used to fund a trust by investing in stocks, bonds, mutual funds, real estate, businesses or cash. They can be saved inside an insurance policy, an investment account, a retirement account, in real estate, a business or a bank account. This book looks at the differences between investing in a taxable investment account compared to insurance policies. The goal is to help you understand the best way for your family to create money in the future to pay for the highest quality of life for your family member with special needs.

Most of the time, we recommend families use term life insurance and invest their savings and long-term money outside of insurance policies. Money invested outside insurance has more potential for growth, it is more accessible in case of emergencies and it is easier to understand how it is invested. Families need to focus on getting out of debt, building emergency funds and investing for the future. Term insurance gives you the time to build a strong financial life without fear of financial ruin.

After reading this, you will have a better understanding of how much life insurance you need, what type to buy and what type of agent to look for to help you. You will also be clear about your reasons for which type of insurance you have – and how much the emotion of caring for your family member might lead you to buying the wrong kind of insurance.

Take care of your family with this important Building Block of your financial foundation.

1

PROTECT YOUR FAMILY

Do you have enough money?

Can your family survive without you?

Is your family's financial future at risk?

What steps have you taken to protect the quality of life of your family members with special needs?

There are critical actions you can take today to reduce the stress caused by gaps in your financial world. Eliminate debt. Build cash reserves. Save for retirement. Update your will and estate plan. Invest to fund a special needs trust.

And buy life insurance. Today.

Life insurance must be the most unloved financial product available. Not enough people have it and those that do often don't have enough. It is not exciting to talk about. It works when you pass away. But it is one of the most important tools to protect your family and reduce stress.

Families with special needs members buy life insurance to protect the living.

Think about the moment of loss if you were to pass away. Family members need to grieve. They have to have time to handle the emotions of loss. The fear and uncertainty get worse when they face financial misery. Life changes enough when a loved person dies. That stress just gets worse if there is not enough money to continue to pay rent or mortgages, to put food on the table and to pay for therapies, medical visits and the activities of daily life.

Our families have a greater need to have insurance in place than typical families. People with developmental disabilities do not have the same opportunities for independent living and employment as do others. We expect to pay more for our family members with special needs over their lifetimes than we do for our typical family members. We need to save and invest today to pay for those expenses in the future. Life insurance covers the giant hole left if we pass away before creating enough assets to pay for those future expenses.

This topic is one that gets the most uncomfortable silences when I talk with groups of families about my Blueprints process of financial planning. It is difficult to think of our own death. We cannot imagine life for our family member with special needs without us in it.

The toughest group of people is moms of children with special needs. They plan to live forever to make sure they can be there for their children. Unfortunately, good planning includes the worst-case scenarios and a person dying early is one of those. Even the tough mom of a person with special needs must plan.

This book will show how to make sure you have enough coverage, that term insurance is recommended for most families and what other life insurance options are available. The marketplace for insurance is confusing and filled with sales pitches for products that sound good but might not work for your family.

Every parent of a family member with special needs has had someone try to sell them life insurance. Last week, I had an American mother living abroad call me to discuss whether or not she should buy the life insurance product being recommended to her. We had a long conversation about the types of insurance, investing and finding ways to protect her recently born son who has Down syndrome.

She was bewildered with the choices. There are four main types of life insurance, each with its own benefits and downsides, and it is hard to tell where the sales pitch for certain insurance ends and any value begins. The conversation started on her end with a whole life sales pitch, moved to term and then a review of universal life and variable life. Each type has different features, costs and promises. This book hopes to set the different types of policies apart, show real world examples and give you tools to make decisions about how much coverage to get and what type to buy.

Chapter 2 helps you understand the primary reason you need life insurance.

Chapter 3 gives you the tools and a sample study to help you decide how much insurance you need.

Chapter 4 reviews the primary types of insurance available.

Chapter 5 compares the returns and expectations of the different types using a real example.

Life insurance offers protection for the worst time – an unexpected and early death of a mother, father or caregiver. Has your family created enough wealth to care for each family member if you are not there? If not, you need life insurance for your family.

2

WHY LIFE INSURANCE?

Life insurance protects your family. It keeps a roof over your family members' heads, food in their stomachs and allows them to pay for life during a time of extreme family stress. Life insurance provides financial security while family members mourn and handle the emotional loss of losing a parent or spouse.

In my financial practice, I meet with people of all ages and situations. Some are families with a newborn with special needs. Others are about to retire or need care themselves and have adult children with special needs. Whatever their ages, they are looking to find the best ways to provide a safe home, a fulfilling life and appropriate care for their family member with special needs.

Life insurance is a critical element to have in place as they save and invest for the long term to reach their goals. Their need for life insurance changes depending on where they are in their careers, how strong their savings and investment accounts are and how much debt they carry.

Families do not always need life insurance. It is a tool used to protect against unexpected loss while they build other elements of their financial life.

4

There are five main reasons to buy life insurance:

1. Replace income
2. Pay off debts
3. Fund future expenses for a family member with special needs
4. Fund education accounts and other life goals
5. Provide estate tax liquidity

Replace income

Households function when one or both parents are working. The income that a mom or dad takes home pays for food, housing, medical expenses, entertainment and all of the activities of daily life. Without a steady paycheck families suffer. Families following the Blueprints process keep three to six months of family expenses in emergency reserves. Unfortunately, emergency funds do not replace the lifetime of lost wages when someone dies in his or her prime working years. The financial impact of losing even a few years of family income is devastating.

Life insurance is a safety net – a means to replace income by creating a pool of money that can be used each year to keep a house, maintain lifestyle and pay for ongoing medical, therapeutic and recreational expenses. Life insurance can be used to replace the retirement savings that comes out of income. The insurance company pays a lump sum to the family that can be used to replace income.

Pay off debts

Debt payments come from income. They need to be paid even if one working family member passes away. The remaining debt payments crush the ability of a family to live a fulfilling and decent life. Families need to get control of debt and create a plan to eliminate debt from their lives. Before that time, families need life insurance.

The biggest debt is one that takes 15, 20 or 30 years to pay off – the mortgage. Families who buy a house or condominium make a financial calculation that the mortgage, taxes and insurance will be less expensive than renting over time and they will create value in a real estate asset. This usually works unless the mortgage payment is too high or when the family income changes.

Life insurance proceeds can be used to create a pool of money to make mortgage payments or to pay off the mortgage.

Life insurance can be used to pay off other debts too – car loans, student loans, personal loans and credit cards. Families need protection in place during that time they have these outstanding debts.

Fund future special needs expenses

Expenses for people with disabilities do not go away at any age. At 18, your family member likely qualifies for Supplemental Security Income and Medicaid funded benefits. These government programs do not replace the financial support you provide for entertainment, fashion, education, therapy, transportation and more that give your family member with special needs a higher quality of life than the government money supports.

The families I work with look to create an account to fund expenses in the future. They save for these expenses as they do retirement and education. They use small dollars today and invest over time to grow funds available to pay for quality of life in the future.

Life insurance used for special needs planning funds a trust or investment account when an insured person passes away. Those years of savings and investing are lost but are replaced through life insurance. There will be money for a special needs family member in the future with insurance in place when someone dies unexpectedly.

Fund education accounts and other life goals

The loss of a working family member will lead to the loss of savings for future education expenses. Families that expect to contribute to college education look to save into 529 plans and other education savings accounts. Life insurance can be used to fund the education accounts if the family collects a death benefit.

Provide estate tax liquidity

Some families use life insurance to fund an account or trust to pay estate taxes or make estate payments to family members. This is common when families have value in assets that take time to sell - like real estate or private businesses. Life insurance provides cash and gives the family time to make decisions about the other assets without the rush to pay the government. Life insurance death benefits come to a person or an estate without the need to pay income tax on the proceeds.

Some basic vocabulary

Understand a few insurance words. These apply to every type of life insurance: death benefit, premium, insured, owner, beneficiary and underwriting class.

Death benefit. The death benefit is the amount of money paid when the insured person dies. Policies can be for $100,000 or less to $5,000,000 or more.

Premium. The premium is the amount paid each month or year to the insurance company.

Insured. The insured is the person whose life is being insured.

Policyholder (Owner). The owner is the person that owns the policy (this can be a trust, business or individual). The owner does not have to be the insured.

Beneficiary. The beneficiary is the person, trust or organization that gets the money when the insured dies. Do not have your family member with special needs as the beneficiary of any policy. Money for that person will be directed to a special needs trust.

Underwriting class. Underwriting class will determine the amount of premium for the death benefit. People in good health with safe lifestyles and who do not smoke will pay less than those who have health issues, motorcycle race (for example) and smoke.

3

CALCULATE YOUR INSURANCE NEED

How big is the financial hole you leave behind if something happens to you tomorrow? Most of us have no idea the true economic value we bring to our families each day.

Life insurance covers the economic loss incurred by families when a spouse or partner dies. The average household in the United States made $52,000 in 2013 according to the Census Bureau. That is more than $2,000,000 earned over a 40 year work history.

Insurance is used to cover big risks by transferring that risk to the insurance company. Loss of income is the greatest risk as our families depend on our paychecks. The need to pay for the work of a stay-at-home spouse or partner is another enormous risk to financial stability. Outstanding debts can be cleared with life insurance proceeds and accounts can be funded all at once if needed.

The right amount of coverage is the most important decision to make at this time.

This chapter will use an example of a family who needs life insurance to help you understand how to choose the right death benefit.

This chapter shows you how to calculate the amount needed for your family.

The types of insurance will be reviewed in the next chapter but remember that most families will want term insurance. Term life insurance allows a family to spend a small amount each month to gain access to a big benefit in the case of the unexpected and early death of a working family member. This is the recommended type of life insurance as you start to create value in your financial life.

Insurance need for a family

Families with working parents need life insurance. This is true for the income earners and for the stay-at-home family members. The risks are too high if any of the family members dies unexpectedly. Family income needs to be replaced from the income-earning members. There must also be money available to pay for all those jobs taken care of by the stay-at-home parent if that person dies.

This section will give an example of a family to show how much they might need for life insurance coverage. This family has a set of working parents.

Mom earns $40,000 part time as a software engineer. Dad earns $75,000 as a CPA for a local firm. They have two children, ages six and four, and the four-year-old child has a significant developmental disability. Mom and Dad are both 36 years old.

They own a home worth $350,000 and have a mortgage of $300,000. The family has $50,000 in student loans, car loans and credit cards. They have worked hard in their careers and education and now see their income growing. They have not attacked their debt and are just figuring out which steps to take to create, preserve and pass along assets.

There is a special needs trust in place in their wills.

This family can pay their bills, save a small amount for retirement and make a dent in their debt. Their combined take home pay is $7,000 per month after taxes, insurance and the contribution to retirement accounts. They have not gotten serious about paying off their debts but they do not see it as a problem. They have not had a focused plan and like most new parents still starting in their careers they live day to day. There is no coordinated financial plan in place.

Out of this $7,000 they pay $1,500 in mortgage payments plus another $500 per month in taxes and insurance.

They feel stretched but not to the limit. They expect to earn more over the next few years as Dad becomes a partner in his firm and Mom goes back to work full-time. At that point they will make up lost savings for retirement, focus on getting rid of debt and building up emergency funds. At least that's the general idea.

What happens if Dad dies this year? Mom still has debt payments each month of $1,000. She still has to pay the mortgage, taxes and insurance of $2,000 per month. She has to find a way to fund her own retirement, pay education costs and leave some money in a trust for her son with special needs. Her take home pay is $2,000 a month after taxes and retirement savings. She could stop retirement savings and increase her take home pay to $2,800 per month. She has debt payments of $3,500 per month and her salary is not enough to feed and care for her family with this debt and housing cost.

If Mom passes away, Dad does not have enough either. He could scrape by but his debt payments are 50% of his take home pay. Every life activity other than housing, medical and meals will have to go.

This family needs life insurance.

Life insurance will pay Mom a lump sum of money if Dad dies during the coverage period. The death benefit insurance on her husband will pay as much as they contracted for at purchase - $250,000, $500,000, $1,000,000 – whatever they decided they needed and could afford at that time.

Choosing a death benefit for your family

There are a few ways to calculate the amount of life insurance needed. Let's go back to the family scenario.

First, look at Dad's contribution to the family budget. Dad contributed $60,000 to the family budget each year after taxes - $5,000 per month. The family needs to create a pool of money to replace this income.

The simplest formula is to look at the dollar amount needed: $60,000. Then the family needs to look at how long they need that money to be replaced. He is 36 years old and expects to work until 61. That is 25 years. The family needs to have $1,500,000 of term life insurance on Dad today. If he were to pass away the next day, Mom would have $1,500,000 from the insurance company and she could use $60,000 per year to help pay the family expenses.

Dad's take home pay:	$60,000 per year
Number of years to cover:	24 years
Death benefit needed:	$1,500,000

$60,000 x 25 = $1,500,000

This is a simple example and useful as a starting point. The figure changes depending on what families do with the money and what they expect to replace. This example does not show any funding for a trust or education accounts. It does not show paying off debts all at once.

Another option is that Mom could invest the money received. At 5% per year the money would earn $75,000. Mom would not have to touch the death benefit received, as the earnings growth replaces her deceased husband's income.

Some families like the security of retiring all debt with life insurance. The family has $350,000 in debts – mortgage, student loans, cars and credit cards. One option is to use the life insurance to pay off debt and then decide how much extra to purchase to replace income needed after the debt payments are taken out of the family budget.

Other families increase the amount of insurance if they expect to add other lifetime expenses into the pool of money. The pool could be used for any expenses imagined – like prepaying college education or funding a trust for future special needs related expenses.

Single parents need life insurance as well. The financial issues do not change and the children at home and person with special needs still have to be protected.

Determine the amount for your family

Calculate the need for your family. Figure out how much coverage you need for each working family member including a stay-at-home parent. Add up your debts. Decide what expenses need to be funded for each member of your family if income is lost.

1.   Start with the take home pay of one family member. Add any amounts withheld pre-tax from the paycheck that are used to pay for health insurance, contributions to retirement accounts and any medical savings accounts. Multiply that number by the number of years that person expects to work.

Add the following and multiply by number of years needed:

Take home pay   _____
plus
expenses paid through
payroll deduction   _____
times
number of years   _____
equals

total for
first family member   _____

For example: $5,000 per month take home pay plus $500 pre-tax medical costs and 401(k) contribution adds up to $5,500 per month. This is $66,000 per year. Multiply that times 25 years equals $1,650,000.

2.   Make the same calculation for the second working family
        member.

Add the following and multiply by number of years needed:

Take home pay   _____
plus
expenses paid through
payroll deduction   _____
times
number of years   _____
equals

total for
second family member   _____

2a. Use this section for a stay-at-home parent instead of the worksheet for the second working family member.

Add the following and multiply by number of years needed:

Day care   _____
plus
respite care   _____
plus
transportation   _____
plus
home activities   _____
plus
other expenses
times
number of years   _____
equals

total for
stay-at-home parent   _____

For example: $30,000 day care plus $5,000 respite care plus $4,000 cleaning plus $6,000 transportation equals $45,000 times 10 years equals $450,000.

Home activities – all the day-to-day work of the stay-at-home parent that needs to be replaced. This includes someone to shop, clean and cook, for example, so the working parent can continue to earn.

3. List all of the family debt outstanding (credit cards, mortgages, loans for cars) that do not end if one person dies. The lender cannot collect student loans when the person who owes the money passes away most of the time.

Mortgage balance   _____
plus
car loan   _____
plus
car loan   _____
plus
credit cards   _____
plus
other debt   _____
equals

outstanding debt   _____

For example: $250,000 mortgage plus $20,000 car loan plus $5,000 credit card plus $25,000 private loan equals $300,000.

4.   Decide the lump sum needed to fund a trust for your family member with special needs.

What will be required to support your family member with special needs? Families with young children with special needs will have to guess at the expenses. Those with older family members with special needs have a track record to use to calculate out of pocket expenses for additional medical and therapeutic treatments, entertainment and more. Use the sample worksheet in Appendix #1 to write down the costs. Multiply expected annual expenses by the number of years needed.

Future special needs
expenses per year   _____
times
number of years   _____
equals

amount needed
for special needs expenses _____

For example: $5,000 transportation expense plus $5,000 medical expense plus $5,000 other expense equals $15,000. This will be needed for 25 years. $15,000 times 25 equals $375,000.

5.   Write down the sum needed to fund other family members' goals.

Do you expect to pay for college at a public school or private? Do you plan to pay for weddings, cars or a down payment towards a first home? Add the expense and multiply by number of years.

College tuition per year x 4 _____
plus
wedding costs   _____
plus
other desired payments   _____
equals

amount needed for
other family expenses   _____

For example: $20,000 tuition times four years equals $80,000. Wedding cost contribution of $10,000. Combined equals $90,000.

Find the total amount of insurance needed for each person by adding your income replacement (#1 or #2) to #3, #4 and #5.

Total insurance on you

_____

Total insurance on spouse or partner

_____

Too much insurance?

This is the most insurance you could need at this time. Your goals and savings will change over time so review this every five years. This is the amount needed if want to cover every imaginable scenario and assume no growth on the money.

There are two other considerations to make when deciding how much insurance to buy.

First, remember inflation. Each year, expenses increase and we have to think about inflation. Over the last decade, inflation has been very low – under 3% per year. 30 years ago, inflation was much higher. Education and health care costs have risen closer to 6% per year. One option is to increase the insurance coverage by some amount to handle inflation.

Second, the money received by the family should be invested if the insurance benefit is paid. Conservative investing will cover inflation. Ideally, some or most of this money is invested for the long-term and can create additional resources. Planning to invest the money decreases the amount of coverage you will need.

There are many good financial planners who can work with you or online financial calculators to help you refine your insurance need after establishing what you want to use the insurance proceeds to protect.

Families that cannot afford the full amount of insurance coverage with a term policy will back in to the amount of coverage they can afford. Do not buy more than you can afford. Review your coverage in five years. You will be able to buy more once you are out of debt and started your savings plan unless you have had a serious health emergency or lifestyle change.

Do not underestimate yourself

Clear your head of the beliefs you have about how much life insurance you need to protect your family. Many people I meet with cannot believe the amount of insurance it takes to protect their families. They have a number in mind that seems like enough. The number is never enough. They look at the total need, whether it's

$100,000, $500,000 or $3,000,000, and it seems like more money than they could ever imagine having at one time.

They have never looked at the value of their income. They have never tallied up their debts. They have never understood that investing each month can add up to hundreds of thousands or millions of dollars over time. They have never seen themselves as people with financial stability.

You will reduce your stress and fear about the future knowing you have taken a key step to protect your family. Hopefully, the death benefit is never paid. There is no need to buy more than is needed. Do not fall into the trap of covering yourself for far less than you are worth.

4

UNDERSTAND POLICY CHOICES

Life insurance choices lead to confusion.

Where should you buy? You can buy life insurance through agents of insurance companies, at online specialists, through your home insurance company, independent brokers and your bank.

What types are available? There are many different types with different names with different features.

How much will you pay? Prices are never displayed when searching online.

What steps happen in what order to get coverage?

This chapter breaks down the main types of life insurance and walks you through how they work. Look for an independent broker with access to many companies when you look to purchase life insurance as that person will help you price and review multiple offerings. You pay the same for the same policy whether you buy it through an online broker or a live person. Rates are set by insurance companies and filed with states. They cannot be changed or added to by brokers or agents.

There are two main types of life insurance: term insurance and "permanent" insurance.

Term insurance covers you for a specific period of time – a term. You pay a premium and hope you do not need the insurance during that time period. Some people call this pure life insurance. You pay for the death benefit only.

Permanent insurance mixes the pure life insurance of term with an "investment" account. Part of the premium goes to a "cash value" account that is similar to a savings or investment account. There are several types of these policies that I call Potential Cash Value policies, PCV for short.

PCV policies break into three main types: whole life, universal life and variable universal life. The types will be explained in this chapter.

You need to know the differences in these policy types when it comes to buying your insurance. Term will give you the most coverage for the least amount of money. PCV policies rarely have a place in planning for families with a special needs member.

Term insurance

Term life insurance is the purest form of life insurance. The insured applies for a certain death benefit then goes through an underwriting process where health and lifestyle history are reviewed. Once approved the policy owner pays a premium each month or year until the end of a certain time period (the term). This is similar to home or car insurance – you pay the premium in the hopes it is never needed.

Term insurance is broken down into a few pieces.

First, the term. How long do you want to have life insurance in place? The term is the time period of coverage. 20-year term is the most common time period of coverage for the people I work with although you can buy 10, 15 or 30-year terms as well.

We use insurance to cover large risks – like the loss of income or to pay off debts. At the start of your planning, risks are high. Young people have a long work life in front of them and need to be covered for most of their working lives. Families with mortgages need to have a pool of money to pay off the mortgage or to use to make payments.

Families following the Blueprints Building Blocks seek to improve their financial lives quickly. 20 years gives them plenty of time to pay debt, build reserves, save for retirement, fund accounts for special needs expenses and get education plans in place.

Life is very different at the end of 20 years for families serious about their financial lives. They have a home with far more equity than debt. They have assets in a variety of investment and retirement accounts. Children who were tiny are now getting ready to move out. The timeline to retirement is far shorter than at the beginning of the term.

20 years is enough time to get the fundamental building blocks of a strong financial life in place.

In my practice, we ladder life insurance policies for some clients. 20 years might not be enough if other children are planned, if savings plans start late or if there is a fiscal emergency along the way. Review insurance needs every five years and adjust the coverage if needed. You can apply for more term insurance if it takes longer than expected to build funds and create wealth.

Families with young children and a family member with special needs might want to look at a 30-year term insurance policy to give them more time to create assets to fund a trust in the future. This adds an additional level of security to a financial plan.

Second, choose a death benefit. How much insurance do you need? The death benefit in a term insurance policy does not change over the term. If you pass away while covered your family (or trust, estate or charity) receives the death benefit. The death benefit ends at the end of the term period or if you stop paying your premium.

Third, the premium. Term insurance premiums give you the chance to buy much more insurance death benefit for lower premiums than buying PCV policies. With term, you pay for insurance and know what you pay.

Most of the time, premiums are level over the term period. The insured pays the same dollar amount in year one as in year 20 in a level premium term policy. Other policies have an increasing premium. Premiums go up each year. They look lower than level term at the beginning and higher later. Level term and increasing premiums tend to average out over the time period and you will pay about the same over 20 years either way.

Potential cash value policies

The other type of insurance has many names – I call them Potential Cash Value policies (PCV). These have the potential to have cash value that you could use at some point in the future. You might hear them referred to as "permanent policies." They are not guaranteed to create cash value. PCV policies will not pay the death benefit if you stop paying the premium or if the cash values fall too low.

These fall into three main types – whole life, universal life and variable universal life. Each will be explained in this chapter and the next. The basic difference between whole, universal and variable universal is how the cash value can grow. There are two goals of PCV policies – to guarantee a death benefit to the family at any time whether in one year or 100 years and to create a fund to use for expenses in the future.

The basic process of buying insurance does not change whether you buy a PCV policy or term. Decide the amount of death benefit you need at a premium you can afford.

These types of policies have some additional parts to understand that separate them from term: cost of insurance, death benefit, surrender charges, guaranteed assumptions and cash value.

Cost of insurance. The cost of insurance in a term policy is the premium. PCV policy insurance costs can be hard to find. They are not always included in illustrations. The cost of insurance inside a PCV policy usually increases each year for each dollar of insurance coverage. It is based on the age of the insured after the policy is issued. The cost of insurance will be low in the first years compared to the end. This cost can be paid by the premium or deducted from cash values.

Death benefit. This is the same definition as with term insurance – the amount purchased is the original death benefit and is paid to the beneficiary of the policy. Unlike term insurance, the death benefit can increase in a PCV policy if the cash values gain substantially. The death benefit in a PCV policy includes the amount in the cash value – it is not the death benefit plus cash values that get paid.

Surrender charges. Policies that have accumulated cash will show a cash value amount and a surrender value amount. The first 10 or 15 years of policies have a surrender charge. This charge recoups the expenses of the insurance company such as commissions and underwriting. After the surrender period is over, the cash value will be the same as the surrender value. Until then, surrender charges reduce the cash available to the policyholder if they want to access any money in the policy.

Guaranteed assumptions. Insurance companies show a worst-case scenario in each illustration for a PCV policy. These show the maximum costs they can charge to the policy and the minimum return. Illustrations also show current assumptions. It is rare for insurance companies to charge the maximum costs.

Cash value. PCV policies have accounts that can gain in value. These accounts help offset the rising costs of insurance. The insurance company has less money at risk as the amount of cash value reduces the amount of pure insurance.

The difference between whole life, universal life or variable universal life policies is how the cash values can grow. There are two goals with PCV policies. The first is to guarantee a death benefit to the family whether you live one year or 100 years from the time you get the policy. The second is to create a fund to use for expenses in the future.

The cash accumulation inside the policy is not as important for families with a special needs member as the death benefit. At some point, these policies will have money that you could take out to use for any purpose. This is the cash value. Money left in the policy has the chance to grow. It will grow tax-deferred while inside the policy.

The main reason the cash values matter is that they help to keep the insurance costs down over the life of the policy. The insurance company has less at risk as your cash values grow. By the end of your life, a significant amount of money returned to your family will be from the money you contributed and its earnings.

Understand the basics of the three different types of policies. There will be an example of the different premium amounts, potential death benefits and life insurance comparing term (and investing), whole life, universal life and variable universal life.

Whole life

Whole life insurance seeks to provide life insurance over your whole life – hence the name. Whole life usually has the highest premium for the same death benefit as the other types of life insurance. Along with the higher premium comes a higher level of guarantee from the insurance company that the death benefit will be there in the future. The premium is not considered flexible in whole life insurance. It will be paid every year at the level determined when you put coverage in place.

Part of the premium goes to a cash value account. This cash value grows by a credit to the account from the insurance company. This credit rate is not predictable and is subject to the ability of the insurance company to pay. The insurance company takes in premiums from policyholders. They invest that money as they see fit. Some portion of the return they generate is credited back to the policyholder. The company also reviews their mortality costs – how many people died that required payout. If this amount is less than expected or needed to pay people then some portion of the leftover amount is credited to policyholders. Essentially, the insurance company returns some of its profit to policyholders in the form of an interest credit.

At death, the benefit paid can be the initial face amount applied for, or even more. These policies will increase in death benefit if the returns of the credit rate lead to an increase in the cash value. Remember, the benefit paid is not the death benefit plus the cash value – it is the death benefit only. Much of the death benefit paid will be the policyholder's own money in the end.

Universal life

Universal life policies give the policyholder more flexibility to pay premiums than in whole life. It was created with the same goal in mind as whole life – to have insurance in place for life. These policies have more clarity about the costs of insurance paid in any given year than do whole life policies. These usually have strong guarantees in place as well.

Cash values in universal life can grow by an interest rate. The insurance company guarantees a minimum interest rate at the time of purchase. Policies have a current interest rate that usually pays more than the minimum. Today, most policies pay somewhere near or above 4%. The guaranteed rate in many policies is closer to 2%. New types of universal life create opportunities for increased gains using indexed annuity options. These have a bit more fluctuation in the cash values but do not change the underlying insurance rates or protections.

Families with special needs should consider "guaranteed" universal life policies if choosing a PCV policy. These tend to have lower premium requirements than whole life insurance and similar death benefit protection. As with whole life, the death benefit can increase.

Variable universal life

Variable universal life is a form of universal life. These policies allow for flexible premium payments. The variable refers to the way the cash values are invested.

The policyholder decides how the cash value gets invested. The policies have sub-accounts (similar to mutual funds) from which the policyholder directs the investment of the cash value. These can be invested conservatively or aggressively depending on the choice of the policyholder. These values fluctuate with the markets.

The variability can work in favor of or against the needs of the policyholder. Good market returns mean that the cash values increase faster than policy expenses. This could lead to a reduction in premiums in the future or increased death benefit for the beneficiary. Of course, the opposite is true. Poor market returns could mean the owner needs to pay more premiums to keep the coverage in place.

These days, people can buy "guaranteed" variable universal life products giving the upside potential of investing with the guarantees of universal life insurance. The guarantee comes with higher insurance expenses than a typical variable policy.

How to decide which policy?

The biggest decision in buying life insurance starts with how much coverage is needed and for how long? The coverage piece you have in place from the work you did in Chapter Two. The time horizon for coverage becomes harder to determine for families with a special needs member.

Typical families look to have insurance in place until they are out of debt, have funded retirement accounts and become empty nesters. Families with a special needs member plan for a longer time horizon. My daughter with Down syndrome might live independently as an adult. She will still need financial support from me as her earnings potential will be lower than for my typical children. She will get government income through Supplemental Security. Her housing and some medical expenses will be supported by Medicaid-funded services. Those government programs will not be enough to provide a high quality of life for her. I will need to have money ready for her when she is 25, 45, 65 and longer – while I am alive, after I pass away and available in the event I do not live to my full life expectancy.

Should I have term insurance or some form of potential cash value life insurance? The emotion in me says some form of "permanent" insurance. The numbers guy in me says term insurance. The experience of working with families says term insurance.

Start with term insurance. You can add or change insurance down the road. Here are the main reasons to start with term insurance and why you will not likely ever need the other type.

1. Affordability. The goal of insurance is to cover risks you cannot cover on your own. Lost income cannot be replaced if you pass

away. Debts still need to be paid. You need the most amount of coverage to fund lost wages and required payments. Term life insurance premiums are small compared to the other types.

2. Timeline of need. Most families do not need life insurance in place forever. Insurance fills the gaps caused by debt, lack of savings, not having investment accounts and poor planning. Families with a special needs member need to get focused on their financial lives so they can help each family member live a fulfilling life. The gaps can be filled with a plan to reduce debt, save for emergencies and fund long-term accounts. 20 years is enough time to get this in place.

3. Investments tend to outperform insurance. PCV insurance policies take your money, charge insurance and investment costs, and return some amount to you as an increase in cash values. Over time, these costs within the policies reduce the future value you could have created on your own. Find a fiduciary-based investment advisor and use that excess premium to invest outside insurance.

4. Experience. Every year, new people come to me to figure out how to get out of their whole life policies. They do not want to pay premiums, they cannot afford their premiums or they no longer need the insurance. So far, I have not seen a policy that lived up to the initial expectations. So far, the additional premium above term would have been treated as well or better in a savings account rather than go to the cash values in the PCV policy. The policies I have seen have cash values barely above the total premiums paid. The death benefits were below the results they would have had by investing the premium in a conservative mix of stocks and bonds in a taxable account.

So is there a role for PCV policies when a family has a special needs member? The families I work with have expressed the desire to help pay for the quality of life of their family member with a disability. PCV policies are sold with the idea that there is a permanent need for insurance.

Yes, there is a limited role for PCV policies. It is at the end of the Blueprints process and only if a few conditions can be met. PCV policies should not be considered until a person is out of debt, has a decent level of money in retirement accounts and is putting money towards growing other assets and investments.

Remember - buy term first. Get coverage in place. Use small dollars to get large amounts of protection.

Once you have a strong financial life in place, then you can decide whether to add a PCV policy. There are a few criteria to meet before considering such a policy. Uncertainty in any area means you should wait.

1. Can you pay more than the target premium? Universal and variable universal life policies allow you to pay more than the target premium. The additional funds go right to the cash value or investment account. You prepay some of the premium that would have to be paid for life. This reduces the risk that you stop paying the premium and lose your guarantees in the policy.

2. Will you need the money? Do not buy a PCV policy and then spend expected premiums and cash values on something other than the insurance – like a new car, boat or trip.

3. Will your family member with special needs outlive you by a decent period of time? Many of our family members have health issues that will shorten life expectancy. Many families have children with fragile health and there is no need for a PCV policy to be purchased. The parents will likely outlive the child. The money is invested better outside of an insurance policy as it can be used to pay for costs of special needs at any time.

There are three reasons why you might consider a PCV policy.

1. Inability to save. Term insurance works best when you save and invest for future needs in an investment account. You have a choice to make when buying life insurance. Pay a smaller premi-

um for term insurance or a larger one for a PCV policy. A PCV policy will cost far more than a term policy. Will you take a portion of the savings from buying term and invest for the future? Will you use that difference to pay off debts and move your financial life forward? If not, you might be best off in a PCV policy where you have to make the premium payment or lose your insurance coverage. Some people need the added incentive of a PCV policy to save.

2. Life expectancy. Insurance companies issue policies based on health and life expectancy at the time of issue. They insure large groups of people and have amazing statistics used to predict life expectancy. You will pay more to have coverage if you have health issues or you might be denied coverage completely. PCV policies have a window of time where they look better financially than when you buy term insurance and use other money to invest. This window tends to be years 30-45 of a policy. Compare these options and if you have some reason to expect a shorter life expectancy than statistics say you might want to consider a PCV policy. This reason flies in the face of the logic of the insurance company's underwriting team but is a real fear expressed by clients.

3. Emotion. The numbers are in favor of buying term insurance. If you cannot get past the fact that you are likely better off buying term, getting out of debt and building other assets, then go ahead and buy something else. If you do, look to buy a guaranteed universal life policy with a good company and keep your premium as low as possible.

A quick word about taxes

Taxes matter. Income taxes reduce take home pay. Investment taxes reduce wealth. Estate taxes can be high. Ideally, you want to invest in a way that minimizes taxes.

Investment accounts owe tax each year on income generated or capital gains taken unless there are offsetting losses. PCV insurance policies defer taxes on income and growth and the death benefit will not be income taxed.

PCV buyers are dazzled with the tax benefits of life insurance. The one-two punch of emotion and tax benefits convince many people that they should start with a PCV policy and only use this type of insurance.

But is it true that the tax benefits add any long-term value? Or does the expense of the PCV policy take away from the tax benefit?

The next chapter will show comparisons of value created in a taxable investment account compared to the different types of PCV insurance policies. These comparisons include taxes taken out of the investment account. The results show that families are still better investing outside of PCV insurance even after paying taxes. The tax benefits do not outweigh the costs of the policies.

5

POLICIES IN ACTION

The emotions of our situations lead us to want to buy PCV policies. We want coverage for our entire lives. But does it make economic sense? This section compares scenarios. You make the decision.

Scenario 1 means buying term insurance and investing the rest in a moderate growth portfolio in a taxable investment account.

Scenario 2 runs a whole life policy and shows the premiums paid throughout the life of the policyholder.

Scenario 3 runs a universal life policy and shows the premiums paid throughout the life of the policyholder.

Scenario 4 runs a guaranteed variable universal life policy and shows the premiums paid throughout the life of the policyholder.

These scenarios use the premium cost assumptions built in to the most expensive insurance option– the whole life policy. The premium here is used as a guideline to review the other types of policies. It gives us a starting point on the maximum premium to pay.

The 36-year-old woman used in the example is looking for $1,000,000 of life insurance. She needs $600,000 to replace income, $300,000 to cover the mortgage, $50,000 for other debt and $50,000 for additional special needs expenses.

She does not smoke and is eligible for the best underwriting health class. What happens if she prices the four different styles of insurance? Let's take a look.

Term insurance and an investment account

This scenario starts with the purchase of a 20-year term insurance policy. The policy will cost $400 per year per a recent quote. She will pay $8,000 for the cost of insurance over 20 years. By comparison, the whole life quote was $11,348 for one year.

The next step is to fund an investment account. She will have $10,948 per year to invest. This is the amount that remains by buying term insurance. $11,348 was the whole life premium. $400 for term insurance. She will take the money saved on the lower premium and invest with a fiduciary advisor.

Assume the money returns 7% per year on average over her life – a moderate long-term expectation. This money sits in a taxable account and she will owe the government some money each year as a result of income paid out and capital gains taken. The taxable gain is 20% of the portfolio and that is taxed at a rate of 25%.

At the end of five years this account has $66,678.52 of value. There is still an insurance need. The family has the $1,000,000 of term insurance in place on her to cover lost income and future expenses.

At the end of 10 years the account has $158,679.03.

At the end of 20 it has $460,763.32.

At this point, 20-year term insurance goes away. The term is over. The investment account has just over $460,000. The initial amount of insurance was $1,000,000.

Was term insurance a good buy at this point or is there still a need?

What else happened over this 20 year time period? The family had a 30-year mortgage of $300,000 at 4%. They now have a mortgage balance of $141,000 as they made regular payments. If they made extra payments the mortgage could be gone. They now have an additional $159,000 in home equity even if the house did not gain in value. The $1,000,000 need was just cut down by $159,000.

The family paid off their debts in the first few years. $50,000 of debt replacement need is gone.

They do not need to replace income for as many years. The 36-year-old woman now is 56 and much closer to retirement. The income replacement gap shrunk by 80%. The income replacement figure was $600,000 at the beginning of the term. It is now $120,000. The insurance need was reduced by another $480,000. (This is the simple math of her take home pay. She brought home $24,000 per year and now has five years of income left to replace).

They have saved an additional $50,000 to fund the expenses for their special needs family member.

The two biggest reasons for the insurance are gone. The family now has $460,000 of investments to replace the insurance. The insurance need dropped to $261,000 - the remaining income needed of $120,000 plus the mortgage balance of $141,000. This is less than what they have in the investment account.

The insurance gap is gone over the 20 years. Most likely, the woman is still alive. She is 56 years old and statistically would expect to live 25 to 35 more years. The next decades improve the picture even more.

At the end of 30 years the investment account has $1,035,854.53. The woman is now 66 years old and likely to still be in good health.

At the end of 40 years the investment account has more than $2,100,000 and at the end of 50 years the account has more than $4,200,000. This puts her at age 86. She contributed $437,920 to the account.

Life insurance companies can price term insurance so low as they use typical life expectancies and spread their risk over large numbers of people. A healthy 36-year-old woman will likely live until her mid-80s. She is not likely to die during the time period of the term.

The biggest financial risk to caring for her family comes in those early working years. At retirement, she should have created enough funds to care for herself and her family member with special needs by staying out of debt, saving in her retirement account and investing in a balanced portfolio for future expenses.

Use these numbers to compare to the PCV life insurance in the next examples. These figures represent the growth in value of the investment account over time.

	Account Value	Total Investment
Year 5 –	$66,678.52	$54,740
Year 10 -	$158,679.03	$109,480
Year 20 -	$460,763.32	$218,960
Year 30 -	$1,035,854.53	$328,440
Year 40 -	$2,130,681.10	$437,920
Year 50 -	$4,214,950.86	$547,400

Whole life

Whole life policies gain in value when the insurance company credits an amount to the policy cash value. The example below uses the mid-point expectations of a current policy illustration.

The whole life policy did not create the same value over time as the investment account. The following are projected cash values from a policy illustration using $1,000,000 of death benefit and an annual premium of $11,348. By the end of year 50 she will have paid $567,400 in premium. The PCV policies have two pieces to review – the death benefit and the surrender value. Surrender value is the cash available in the policy less any payments due to the insurance company. This is the money that can be taken out at any time. The death benefit is the insurance coverage.

The first column shows surrender value, the second the death benefit. The third column shows total premiums paid.

	Surrender	Death Benefit	Premium Paid
Year 5 –	$28,774	$1,001,964	$56,740
Year 10 -	$95,309	$1,013,077	$113,480

Year 20 -	$255,898	$1,083,214	$226,960
Year 30 -	$493,696	$1,223,901	$340,440
Year 40 -	$822,938	$1,406,456	$453,920
Year 50 -	$1,254,117	$1,655,361	$567,400

The cash value in the whole life policy is close to $3,000,000 less in value than the projected value of the investment account at age 86. The death benefit is about $2,500,000 less than the amount in an investment account. Remember also how much of the owner's money is in the policy. The owner has put $567,400 of premium into the policy to get returned $1,655,361 as a death benefit. A third of her own money is being repaid.

As with all the PCV insurance types here, there is a window where these policies work better than buying term insurance and putting money into investment accounts. Each of the PCV policies look better when the insured dies somewhere around 30-45 years after the policy is issued. This is a small window of outperformance but it is worth reviewing.

Universal life

Universal life policies use an interest rate to credit account values. Illustrations show a guaranteed interest rate and a current interest rate that provide some idea of how the cash values could grow over time.

Universal life and variable universal life products have one significant advantage over whole life products. You control your premiums. For the most part, whole life requires payment at a set premium for the life of the policy to get the benefit paid. The universal and variable policies give you flexibility on how much premium to pay each year. Another advantage in these types of universal life policies is the transparency of costs. Illustrations can show how much of the premium goes to insurance costs and how much to the cash value account.

The insurance costs in universal life are usually lower than the costs for the same death benefit in a whole life policy. Universal life policies have a target premium that provides the basis of any guarantees. Additional payments above the target premium go to the cash value to earn interest or market returns.

Universal life policies can be "guaranteed." If the target premium is paid each year, then the policy death benefit is guaranteed no matter what the cash value account returns. The premiums for a guaranteed universal life policy are much less than similar premiums for whole life insurance.

One policy reviewed for comparison purposes has a target premium of $3,865. The illustration used shows $11,000 of premium paid, similar to what was paid in the whole life illustration. The amount over the target premium goes to the cash value and has the opportunity to earn the policy interest rate.

The returns in this universal life policy show a credit interest rate of 4.5% for a non-guaranteed policy. Here is how the money grows.

	Surrender	Death Benefit	Premium Paid
Year 5 –	$32,256	$1,000,000	$55,000
Year 10 -	$94,102	$1,000,000	$110,000
Year 20 -	$238,192	$1,000,000	$220,000
Year 30 -	$451,421	$1,606,833	$330,000
Year 40 -	$699,092	$2,459,143	$440,000
Year 50 -	$1,061,964	$3,058,410	$550,000

Again, in 50 years, the PCV policy shows less value than the investment account. The investment account has more than $1,000,000 in value than the death benefit of this universal life policy.

This universal life illustration shows a much higher death benefit than in the whole life illustration.

Variable universal life

Variable universal life policies share the premium flexibility of standard universal life. They differ in that the excess premiums and cash values are invested through separate accounts (similar to mutual funds). The policyholder directs the investment mix.

Currently, there are "guaranteed" variable universal life insurance policies available. Policyholders who pay the target premium throughout the life of the policy will have the insurance in place. Non-guaranteed variable universal life policies are not recommended. The death benefit can be lost if the account values do not grow as expected.

Again, the benefit of these types of policies is the ability to control the premium. You can put in more money than required. The money goes to investments and can grow. The cash values can be used in the future to pay insurance costs inside the policy or be taken out to spend. Increasing cash values can lead to higher death benefits.

Compared to the investment account, the variable life insurance policy does not accumulate the same cash value over a long period of time. It does, however, provide more benefit than either of the other types of PCV policies.

	Surrender	Death Benefit	Premium Paid
Year 5 –	$10,573	$1,606,637	$55,000
Year 10 -	$67,150	$1,661,383	$110,000
Year 20 -	$287,962	$1,852,684	$220,000
Year 30 -	$629,956	$2,194,678	$330,000
Year 40 -	$1,194,996	$2,759,718	$440,000
Year 50 -	$1,910,352	$3,475,074	$550,000

This illustration uses a 6.35% rate of return on the cash values – a higher return than available in the other types of universal life or whole life. This illustration uses a "guaranteed" variable universal life policy. This sample shows the death benefit growing. The premium covers a death benefit of $1,564,722 in the guarantee when the target premium is paid.

The most good with the fewest dollars

Families with a special needs member cannot afford to take risks with their life insurance. Term insurance is a simple, effective way to provide coverage for a family member at the time of greatest need. The most insurance can be bought for the least amount of money with term. Term insurance provides basic coverage – similar to how car or home insurance works.

Insurance is not required to be in place for all years. Saving and investing helps families establish financial independence and security. Wealth accumulation happens over time by paying off debts, building reserves and investing for growth.

PCV insurance policies do have the ability to accumulate value. They can provide assurance and peace-of-mind as there is the chance to have a death benefit at any point in the future. Judge for yourself whether the emotional cost is worth more than the expected value you can create for your family by investing outside of life insurance policies.

6

DECISIONS FOR
YOUR FAMILY

The side-by-side comparisons show that you have the opportunity to create far more value for your family by investing outside of life insurance. The decision is clear to me. Buy term insurance. Invest the difference. Change your behavior to focus on long-term financial health.

The chances of financial success will increase for your family by sticking to a simple investing plan over time. The numbers work in your favor. Your heart and head will be satisfied when you start building wealth that can support your family member with special needs.

Some families cannot let go of the idea of PCV insurance. They get pulled between emotions and the clear math.

If you answer "no" to any of the following questions, buy term insurance. Nothing else. These are clear signals to keep costs for insurance low.

Is all your debt paid off?

Are you fully funding retirement accounts?

Are you accelerating your mortgage payments?

Do you have three to six months of cash reserves?

If you answered "yes" to each question, then you can go through the exercise of looking at PCV policies if you cannot shake the idea that it will be beneficial. Meet with an independent insurance broker who works with many different companies. Review the policies against a reasonable investment return. Understand the surrender charges, the limited access to funds and the risks you take.

There are two reasons why you might want to buy a PCV policy.

One reason is if you do not trust yourself to save and invest for the long-term. You do not think you will stick to the plan and invest well. A solid investment advisor and financial planner can help you over this hurdle but buy insurance if you need and want the guarantees. Understand the cost you pay and move ahead anyway.

The other is where your emotion overrides the evidence in front of you. You focus on those years where returns in PCV policies outpace investing even though you know you will likely outlive this window.

If either of these reasons fits you, then buy some version of a guaranteed universal life policy. Contribute as much as you can in the first years of the policy to reduce the risk of losing the policy in the future. Plan to pay premiums for a long time.

Love and protect your family

My financial planning process for families with special needs member is called Blueprints. There are key Building Blocks to follow designed to help you provide the best life possible for your family member with special needs. Take time to dream about the future. Organize your financial life. Meet with an attorney to put a special needs trust in place. Get out of debt. Save for your own retirement. Buy term life insurance.

Insurance products – life, health, disability, long-term care, home and auto – reduce the risk of huge mistakes. You know your family will survive in their financial life by having a safety net in place.

Remember, life insurance is not for you. Life insurance protects every member of your family. In the process, you do something for yourself. You reduce the stress and anxiety of not knowing what happens to your family if you pass away.

Buying life insurance is a quick event as you build your financial life. This important step needs to happen and you will feel a huge weight lifted from your shoulders by contacting an independent broker and starting the process today.

Appendix 1

Sample Budget Worksheet

Use this worksheet to calculate the life insurance need for future expenses for your family member with special needs. Families with adult children with special needs will have a history of payments to work with to make their calculations. Families with young children will make a best guess and then review these numbers in the future.

Some expenses happen each month. Multiply these by 12 to get an annual number. Some expenses happen once per year. Do not forget to write these down. We tend to forget expenses made more than a month ago. Write down how many years these expenses will need to be paid. Multiply the expenses with numbers of years.

Others happen infrequently. It might be a piece of medical equipment, an expected procedure or a special trip. Write these down. If they happen more than once figure for how many years the expenses will be paid.

Add the infrequent and regular expenses and use that number to include in your life insurance calculations.

Protect Your Family Budget Worksheet

	Monthly Expense	Annual Expense	Infrequent Expense
Supplemental Medical	_____	_____	_____
Supplemental Therapy	_____	_____	_____
Cable/Satellite/Phone	_____	_____	_____
Clothing	_____	_____	_____
Education	_____	_____	_____
Entertainment	_____	_____	_____
Fitness	_____	_____	_____
Taxes	_____	_____	_____
Beauty	_____	_____	_____
Respite	_____	_____	_____
Subscriptions	_____	_____	_____
Transportation	_____	_____	_____
Travel	_____	_____	_____
Medical Equipment	_____	_____	_____
Technology	_____	_____	_____
Special Equipment	_____	_____	_____
Furniture	_____	_____	_____
Auto Expenses	_____	_____	_____
Cleaning/Laundry	_____	_____	_____
Care Assistance	_____	_____	_____
Home Expenses	_____	_____	_____

Appendix 2

Comparisons

The values below are the same ones shown in Chapter 5 – Policies in Action. They are provided here for easy reference.

Table 1 – This table shows the investment account returns compared to the surrender values in the illustrated policies. The cash value equals the surrender value after a period of time in each policy.

Cash Value Comparison

Year	Investment	Whole	Universal	Variable
Year 5	$66,678.52	28,774	32,256	10,573
Year 10	158,679.03	95,309	91,102	67,150
Year 20	460,763.32	255,898	238,912	287,962
Year 30	1,035,854.53	493,693	451,421	629,956
Year 40	2,130,681.10	822,938	699,092	1,194,996
Year 50	4,214,950.86	1,254,117	1,061,964	1,910,352

Table 2 – This table shows the investment account returns compared to the death benefit of the illustrated policies.

Death Benefit Comparison

Year	Investment	Whole	Universal	Variable
Year 5	$66,678.52	1,001,964	1,000,000	1,606,637
Year 10	158,679.03	1,013,077	1,000,000	1,661,383
Year 20	460,763.32	1,083,214	1,000,000	1,852,684
Year 30	1,035,854.53	1,223,901	1,606,833	2,194,678
Year 40	2,130,681.10	1,406,456	2,459,143	2,759,718
Year 50	4,214,950.86	1,655,361	3,058,410	3,475,074

Disclosures

_____

Life insurance quotes

The life insurance quotes in this book came from actual quotes for a 36-year-old woman in the best underwriting class. They are quotes reviewed in April and May of 2015. These illustrations are for educational purposes. They are not made with the intent to sell or distribute life insurance products. Quotes for insurance are subject to change in price. Applicants must go through an underwriting process and are not guaranteed coverage.

Investment returns

The investment returns do not reflect a particular strategy, product, fund or asset allocation. The returns are based on a 7% annual return in each year of investing in a taxable account. 20% of returns are taxed at a 25% tax rate to approximate income, dividends and turnover. They are not guaranteed. They do not represent any form of FDIC protection.

Comparisons

The comparisons used represent what I believe to be achievable investment returns compared with actual life insurance illustrations. The middle level of return and cost was used for the whole life policy. A 4% return was used for the universal life policy and a 6.35% net return (of separate accounts) was used in the variable universal life policy.

ABOUT THE AUTHOR

Rob Wrubel, CFP® AIF® is the creator of *Blueprints,* a financial planning process to help families with a special needs member get out of debt, save for retirement and protect and enhance potential government benefits for their family member with special needs. He is a Senior Vice President, Investments with Cascade Investment Group in Colorado Springs, CO.

Rob has three children. His middle child was born in 2003 and she has Down syndrome. A few months after her birth, Rob began to research how financial planning for a family with a special needs member is different than planning for a typical family. He has focused his practice on working with families with special needs members and the professionals and organizations that serve them.

He donates time through his direct support of several organizations. He currently serves as Board Member of the Pikes Peak Community Foundation. He has served as President of the Cheyenne Village Board of Directors and CASA of the Pikes Peak Region. He has served on the Boards of Directors of the Ronald McDonald House Charities of Southern Colorado, the Colorado Fund for People with Disabilities and the Colorado Springs Down Syndrome Association.

Rob is a New Jersey native and graduate of Wesleyan University in Middletown, CT.